SEINFELD TRIVIA

Everything About Nothing

Dennis Bjorklund

D1008384

MAIZELAND BOOKS

This publication is intended to provide accurate and authoritative information about the subject matter covered. It is sold with the understanding that the publisher does not render legal, accounting or other professional services. If legal advice or other expert assistance is required, seek the legal services of a competent professional.

Persons using this publication when dealing with specific legal matters should exercise discretion and their own independent judgment, and research original sources of authority and local court rules and procedures.

The publisher and author make no representations concerning the contents of this publication and disclaim any warranties of merchantability or fitness for a particular purpose, or any other liability for reliance upon the contents contained herein.

This publication is merely the commencement of dialogue with the readers, and we welcome suggestions to update the book for reprint and future editions. Send all comments to the address hereinbelow.

Library of Congress Cataloging-in-Publication Data
Bjorklund, Dennis
        Seinfeld Trivia: Everything About Nothing / Dennis Bjorklund.
                p.   cm
        "A Maizeland Books book"

        1. Seinfeld (Television program)–Miscellaneous.   I. Title.

        First published in the United States of America in 1998

CONTENTS

INTRODUCTION

What started as a passion for quality sitcoms has developed into a passion for making these timeless television classics accessible to the public. *Seinfeld* is one of those all-time great sitcoms, from an age when situation comedies dominated the airwaves; a time before reality TV engulfed the social milieu. The author has written several books on some of the best and most popular television programs. If you are a fan of sitcoms and love some of the most hilariously written dialogue, then you should check out some of the other books on the subject.

Toasting *Cheers*: An Episode Guide to the 1982-1993 Comedy Series

***Cheers* TV Show: A Comprehensive Reference**

***Cheers* Trivia: It's A Little Know Fact . . .**

***Seinfeld* Secrets: An Insider Scoop About the Show**

***Seinfeld* Reference: The Complete Encyclopedia with Biographies, Character Profiles & Episode Summaries**

Seinfeld Ultimate Episode Guide

Seinfeld Trivia: Everything About Nothing

This book was written to commemorate the *Seinfeld* show and provide the reader with some of the most memorable snippets that made this such a widely successful program.

Many people claimed the show was about nothing. Even the creators made fun of this fact, but somewhere within all the nothingness lies truth about everything. *Seinfeld* had a way of discussing some of the trivialities of life that we all take for granted, and spin it into one hilarious episode on the subject.

Seemingly mundane things took on a life of their own. *Seinfeld* exposed the close-talker, the low-talker, how lighting can change someone's appearance, or even incessant dog barking that prevents us from sleeping.

No topic seemed to be off limits. *Seinfeld* delved into virgins, masturbation, contraception (for women and men), pregnancy scares, outing a gay person, and other topics that were taboo on network television, at the time. The NBC censors were always bussing about the show and quick to prevent overtly mentioning certain words or phrases.

Thus, the subject of being gay always had the tag line, "not that there's anything wrong with that." The subject of masturbation never mentioned the word, but the gang bragged how they were "master of their domain." Even touchy subjects of how a guy "took IT out" during a date, never mentioned the word "penis." The censors laid down the law, but the *Seinfeld* creators always found a way around it. They worked tirelessly in the "gray areas" of the censorship law.

It is this type of creativity and humorous twists to everyday events that made the show a hit. But it was not simply the younger generation that liked the show. The older folks also liked it because *Seinfeld* added a great supporting cast of recurring regulars to play the parents of Jerry and George. Not only were they great actors, but their delivery often made them "scene-stealers" in many episodes. Anyone who thinks about past episodes cannot help but remember some of the insanely funny yelling tirades between George's mother and father. Although Jerry's parents were more subdue, his father was quirky enough to garner attention and his mother's incessant nosiness we can all relate to.

Even the extended family and neighbors made the show memorable. Who can forget Uncle Leo and his jocular, "Hellooo!" or Babu saying that Jerry is a "very, very bad man," and I can still hear Jerry say, "Newman!" in his devilish voice. But the real glue that held the show together was the cast.

George, Kramer and Elaine made the show. They played off Jerry's average-guy routine to deliver some unforgettable lines. George's vociferous rants (the apple did not fall far from the tree), Elaine's thrusting push when she was astounded as she says, "Get Out!" And of course, Kramer's eccentricities (to put it mildly) and hipster move each time he entered Jerry's apartment. I am sure everyone reading this Introduction can picture each episode when these events occurred.

That is what made *Seinfeld* so special and timeless. To any fan, simply throw out a line or phrase, and instantly everyone in the group will know what you are taking about..The goal of this book is to bring back some of those memories; to allow you to escape and relive the jocularity of the show; but also, to test your cognitive recollection. Read on, and see if, in the realm of *Seinfeld*, you are Master of Your Domain.

SCORING

Correct Answers	*Seinfeld* Skill Level
300-333	Master of Your Domain
250-299	King of the County
200-249	Queen of the Castle
150-199	The Wiz
100-149	Not Spongeworthy
50-99	Hipster Doofus
0-49	*Seinfeld* Virgin

Chapter One

The Show

Questions

1.   Name the two creators of *Seinfeld*?

2.   The *Seinfeld* characters live in which city?

3.   What is the street address where Jerry and Kramer's apartment is located?

4.   What is the real-life business name of the diner where the *Seinfeld* gang often meets?

5.   Name the song title and musical artist who popularized this establishment in a 1990 hit?

6. Which *Seinfeld* character was not originally included in the pilot episode?

7. Who is the real life inspiration for the George Costanza characters?

8. Who is the real life inspiration for the Cosmo Kramer character?

9. In the pilot episode, Jerry's neighbor was not named Kramer. What was his neighbor's original name (before it was changed to Kramer)?

10. On which night of the week did *Seinfeld* have its best rating success?

11. What is the "dating loophole"?

12. What conversational topic linked the first and last episode?

Answers

1.   Jerry Seinfeld and Larry David.

2.   New York City.

3.   129 West 81st Street, Manhattan. This was where Jerry once lived. However, the exterior views in each episode are from a Los Angeles apartment building.

4.   Tom's Restaurant.

Larry David

5. "Tom's Diner" by D.N.A. featuring Suzanne Vega.

6. Elaine. Her character was added after the pilot episode received low ratings.

7. The co-creator, Larry David. He based the character upon himself.

8. Kenny Kramer. He was Larry David's neighbor.

9. Kessler.

10. Thursday.

11. When a guy makes an outlandish bet he is sure to lose, and the bet is to buy the woman dinner. It is a guaranteed date.

12. A discussion about the location of a shirt button.

The *Seinfeld* cast (from left: Michael Richards, Julia Louis-Dreyfus, Jerry Seinfeld, and Jason Alexander) perched in front of a New York City skyline.

Chapter Two

Jerry Seinfeld

Questions

1.   In the show, what was Jerry's birth name?

2.   What were the names of Jerry's childhood friends (other than George Costanza)?

3.   Which Super Hero is Jerry's favorite?

4.   Who is Jerry's baseball hero?

5.   What is Jerry's ATM password?

6. When Jerry's jugular was cut, who provided the blood for the transfusion?

7. Why was Jerry denied membership to the Friar's Club?

8. What was the name of the elderly client Jerry volunteered to provide companionship?

9. What was suspicious about Jerry's accountant?

10. Who is Jerry's favorite explorer?

11. If Jerry were abducted by aliens, what job would he like to have?

12. At what high school gym class competition did Jerry win, but his rival Duncan Meyer suspected impropriety?

13. What was Jerry's standard line when asked for a rematch?

14. What was the name of the book that Jerry was 20 years overdue in returning to the library?

15. Where did Jerry attend college?

Jerry (Jerry Seinfeld) wearing the puffy shirt.

16. Where did Jerry and George first meet, and what was special about their first meeting?

17. What was the name of the neighborhood restauranteur to which Jerry offered advice about opening a shop offering an all-Pakistani cuisine?

18. What movie does Jerry consider to be the worst of all-time?

19. What is Jerry's favorite sports team?

20. What was the name of the personal trainer who was hired by Jerry's parents to "whip Jerry into shape"?

21. What medical condition did Jerry claim to have when he was trying to get out of a public urination charge?

22. What was the name of Jerry's auto mechanic (who was also dating Elaine)?

23. Why did Jerry temporarily switch auto mechanics and terminate his relationship with David Puddy?

24. As a struggling comedian, what job did Jerry have to earn money?

25. What was the name of the appliance business that Jerry promoted as a commercial spokesperson?

26. What is the name of the hack comedian to whom Jerry was a mentor?

27. What was the name of the television show that Jerry and George were hired to create, and write a pilot episode?

28. What caused Jerry's girlfriend, the virgin, to breakup with him?

29. What caused Jerry's girlfriend, the Calvin Klein model, to break-up with him?

30. What was the name of the woman whose name rhymed with a part of the female anatomy?

31. What was the name of Jerry's girlfriend who had the special power to get her way with any man?

32. How did Jerry lose Nicki to another man?

33. When Jerry wanted to date his girlfriend's roommate, what was his plan to make the switch?

34. What was the name of Jerry's girlfriend who didn't have a "square to spare"?

35. What was the misunderstanding between Jerry and a reporter who wanted an interview for a school newspaper?

36. What was the name of the woman that Jerry dated who was his exact identical female counterpart?

37. Who's dating relationship was Jerry "waiting out" (waiting for them to break-up)?

38. Which girlfriend shook her head repeatedly and refused to have one taste of apple pie?

39. Who was Jerry "gaga" over, once he discovered that Kramer also liked her, and how did he prove his love to his soul mate?

40. Which girlfriend used the "relationship barometer" and how did he determine how important he was in her life?

41. How does Jerry impress Alex, a woman infatuated with Mexican hairless dogs?

42. As a girlfriend, Lanette was the most exhausting and demanding, so Jerry needs to hire an assistant to keep up with her. Who was Jerry's relationship intern?

43. Celia offered wild sex, but what made Jerry so frustrated every time he was in her apartment?

44. How does Jerry overcome his frustration with Celia?

45. While dating Rachel Goldstein, a nice Jewish girl, what did she and Jerry do that offended both families?

46.   When dating a woman (Sidra) from the health club, Jerry is obsessed with which part of her anatomy?

47.   When asked if they were real, how did Sidra describe her breasts to Jerry?

48.   What was the name of Jerry's "pretend" wife, and why did he get "fake" married?

49.   When Jerry dated a Romanian gymnast, why were they both disappointed in bed?

Answers

1.   Jerome. He joked that if asked nicely, he would change his name to Claude.

2.   Joel Horneck. Jerry only befriended him because he owned a Ping-Pong table (Jerry claims he would have befriended Stalin if he had a Ping-Pong table).

"Fragile" Frankie Merman. He earned the nickname at summer camp. Whenever he was upset, he would run into the woods, dig a hole, and sit in it.

3.   Superman.

4.   Mickey Mantle.

5.   Jor-El (Superman's biological father).

6.   Kramer. This drove Jerry crazy because he could feel Kramer's blood borrowing things from his blood. Subsequently, when Jerry was dragged behind his car by the Mandelbaum's, he had to get a transfusion from Newman!

7.   A dispute arose over a misplaced dinner jacket. Jerry borrowed a jacket from the club, and offered it to a group performing at the club, and they made it disappear.

8.   Sidney Fields.

9.   He was the sniffing accountant. Kramer convinced Jerry that his accountant, Barry Prophet, had a bad drug habit and was embezzling his money.

10.   Magellan.

11.   He would like to work in the circus because he would get to travel and would still be in show business.

12.   Track.

13.   "I choose not to run!"

14.   *Tropic of Cancer*. He actually loaned the book to George.

15.   Queens College.

16. They met in gym class. Jerry was spotting George as he climbed a rope, but he kept slipping down, and eventually fell on Jerry's head.

17. Babu Bhatt.

18. *Plan 9 From Outer Space.*

19. New York Mets.

20. Izzy Mandelbaum. His memorable catch phrases were, "You think you're better than me?" and "It's go time!"

21. Uromysitisis.

22. David Puddy.

23. Jerry was upset because David Puddy used "The Move" on Elaine. Jerry invented "The Move" and did not want Puddy using it within the city limits.

24. Selling Umbrellas. He proudly boasts that he invented "the twirl."

25.   Leapin' Larry's Wholesale Appliance and Electronics.

26.   Kenny Bania.

27.   "Jerry."

28.   He revealed the masturbation contest that was being held amongst his friends.

29.   The pick. Jerry was accused of picking his nose. He claimed it was in the outer rim.

30.   Delores. Jerry could not think of her name, and once referred to her as Mulva.

31.   Nicki.

32.   Jerry lost Nicki to another man who used the "dating loophole." Todd Gack, Elaine's ex-boyfriend, used ridiculous bets to win a date with a woman. For example, he wagered that Dustin Hoffman was in *Star Wars*. If he lost the bet, Todd would buy the woman dinner.

Jerry's (Jerry Seinfeld) embarrassing jacket liner.

33. He suggested a menage a trois. However, when they were both into the idea, Jerry had to rethink his plan because he is not an orgy guy.

34. Jane. She refused to give Elaine any toilet paper when they were in adjoining stalls because she didn't have a square to spare.

35. She thought Jerry was gay (and George was his life partner). She "outed" him in her article.

36. Jeannie Steinman. They had everything in common and even looked alike. When Jerry realized he found the perfect person (himself), he proposed marriage.

37. Dr. Beth Lookner.

38. Audrey. She was Poppie's daughter.

39. Jane. Jerry proved his love by scheduling a vasectomy because she did not want to have children.

40. Valerie. She used the telephone speed dial as a relationship barometer. Jerry worked hard to get to #1, so Valerie's stepmother fought back to regain the top spot.

41. He starts shaving his chest hairs.

42. George. He was actually a great intern until he was sidetracked by a game of Frolf (Frisbee golf) and forgets to mail invitations for her party.

43. Celia owned a collection of vintage unused toys, and she refused to allow Jerry to play with them.

Jerry Seinfeld on the phone.

44. Jerry gives her medication to make her drowsy so he can play with her toys while she sleeps. He also feeds her turkey, wine, and a healthy dose of Costanza home movies to get her to pass out.

45. They were busted having a heavy make-out session during the movie *Schindler's List*. According to Newman, Jerry was moving on her like the Storm Troopers into Poland.

46. Her breasts. Jerry wanted to know if her breasts were real.

47.   "They're real, and they're spectacular."

48.   Meryl. They married so she could get a discount on dry cleaning.

49.   Jerry was expecting acrobatic sex, and she expecting the best sex ever. In her country, the one man who is supposed to fulfill all sexual desires is known as a comedian. And, according to her, Jerry is no comedian.

Chapter Three

George Costanza

Questions

1. During his childhood, George was raised and lived in which New York City borough?

2. What was the highest rank that George ever attained as a Cub Scout?

3. Name one of the "single most damaging" experiences during George's life.

4. George's childhood bedroom was converted into what type of room by Frank Costanza, George's father?

5.   How did George's mother hurt her back, which required a hospital stay?

6.   Frank Costanza's family immigrated to America from which European region?

7.   Why did Frank Costanza lose all interest in politics and refused to vote?

8.   How tall is George?

9.   Why does George refuse to wear a hat?

10.   According to George, why did Elaine dislike his toupee?

11.   If George is abducted by aliens, where would he want to be confined and why?

12.   Why does George dislike facial hair, and what type of lubricant does he use when shaving?

13.   What fabric does George love so much that he would want to be draped in it?

14. When exacting revenge on someone (his ex-boss) for the first time in his life, what did George do?

15. What was George's most often used fictional name?

16. When George visits a holistic healer, what type of plant does he resemble when being rushed to the hospital?

17. What unique behavior does George exhibit when he uses a bathroom?

18. When George is given $1,900 from a childhood saving account, how does he spend the money?

19. When donating to the blind, what type of currency does George use?

20. What is George's secret ATM password?

21. Who was the first person to be told George's secret ATM password?

22. What is the one secret George will take to the grave?

George (Jason Alexander) using the art of seduction.

23. Just to date a woman, George converted to what religion?

24. Who does George consider to be the most unattractive world leader of all-time?

25. Who is George's favorite explorer?

26. What is George's typical order at Monk's diner?

27. What type of book does George prefer to read in the restroom?

28. George had a memorable game of Trivial Pursuit against which person?

29. According to the Trivial Pursuit card, what was the answer to this question: "Who invaded Spain in the eighth century?"

30. If George was stranded on an island, and he could only choose one book, which one would he choose?

31. Who would George choose as his island companion: Richard, Wilt or Neville Chamberlain?

32. Who is George's favorite actress?

33. When George hit an inside-the-park home run in softball and bowled over the catcher, who was the catcher?

34. George's telephone answering machine is a parody of what popular '70s TV show?

35. When George had to compete against another tenant for a bigger apartment in his building, what heart-wrenching tragedy did the other tenant survive?

36. George purchased a 1989 Chrysler LeBaron when he learned the name of the prior owner. Who was the prior owner?

37. How did George's gym teacher pronounce his last name?

38. George had the high score on what video game machine at Mario's Pizza, his old high school hangout?

39. To win the affection of the "It" girl in college (Diane DeConn), two decades later George pretends to work in what professional field?

40. When George saves a beached whale, what was obstructing its blowhole?

41. George most frequently pretends to be employed in what occupation?

42. Why was George fired from his job as a proofreader for a publishing company?

43. What elaborate lie does George concoct to get a 13-week extension on unemployment benefits?

44. When George was hired as a hand model, his hands were only second-best to what other hand model, and what ended the guy's career?

45. What was George's official position when he was first hired by the New York Yankees?

46. What was the name of George's personal secretary, and why did he hire her?

47. While employed at Play Now (a playground equipment business), what lie did George perpetuate that enraged his employer?

48. What fictitious charity did George invent to avoid exchanging Christmas presents with coworkers?

49. According to George, what is the test to determine if a person is homosexual?

50. What is George's strategy to finagle at least three dates with a woman?

51. Who would George rather date, someone who is blind or deaf, and why?

52. What would be George's porn star name?

53. What fruit gave George a shot of B-12 and enhanced his performance in bed?

54. What was the name of George's deceased fiancee, and how did she die?

55. What name did George reserve for his first child, and whom does it honor?

Answers

1.   Queens.

2.   Webelos. George was stuck at this level for 3 years because he kept losing the Pinewood Derby.

3.   According to George, there were two: 1) Seeing his father naked; and 2) when he broke a statue that he was using as a microphone to sing, "MacArthur Park" (his parents looked at him as if he smashed the ten commandments).

4.   A billiard parlor.

5.   She caught George masturbating in the living room, which caused her to faint.

6.   Tuscany, Italy.

7.   Because he was an immigrant and therefore ineligible to become President of the United States.

8.   5' 6".

9. He was worried about the look of disappointment on a woman's face when she first sees his hairline.

10. Knowing that the toupee brought George confidence, she realized that she lost her chance to have him as a lover.

11. George would like to be confined in the zoo because he could set his own schedule and hopefully he would get a woman so he could mate.

12. Facial hair makes him feel like an out-of-work porn star. George uses butter when shaving.

13. Velvet. He only wishes it was socially acceptable to be ensconced in velvet.

14. He slipped a mickey in the drink of his ex-boss in retaliation for being humiliated at work.

15. Art Vandelay.

16. Eggplant.

17. He takes off his shirt.

George (Jason Alexander) wearing a rat-hair hat.

18. He buys a work of art from a dying artist hoping it will increase in value. Naturally, the artist recovers, leaving George with useless triangles.

19. Coins. George refuses to give paper currency because he wants the blind person to hear his generosity.

20. Bosco.

21. J. Peterman's mother. She was on her dead bed, and the secret was killing George, so he thought it was safe (who was she going to tell in the afterlife).

---

22. His real SAT score. He claims it was 1409 but that is not the truth.

23. Latvian Orthodox.

24. Lyndon Johnson.

25. Desoto.

26. George usually orders tuna on toast, coleslaw, and a cup of coffee.

27. *French Impressionist Paintings*. He finds the pastoral images soothing and conducive to his bowel movements.

28. The Bubble Boy, Donald Sanger.

29. The Moops. It was a typo but George refused to concede defeat when the Bubble Boy answered, "The Moors."

30. *The Three Musketeers*. He never read the book and is saving it for just such an occasion.

31.   George would choose Richard Chamberlain because he was in the movie, *The Three Musketeers*, so George would not have to read the book.

32.   Candice Bergen. Ever since watching *Carnal Knowledge*, she has been George's favorite actress.

33.   Bette Midler. It was a charity softball game against the cast of *Rochelle, Rochelle The Musical*.

34.   "Greatest American Hero." George uses a parody of the song, "Theme From *Greatest American Hero*" by Joey Scarbury. The lyrics start, "Believe it or not, George isn't at home...."

35.   The other tenant, Clarence Eldridge, survived the sinking of the Andrea Doria. George's rebuttal–recounting the tales of Costanza--was equally enthralling.

36.   John Voight. Not the actor; it was John Voight, the periodontist.

37.   Can't Stand Ya.

38.   Frogger.

39. Marine Biology. George pretends to be a marine biologist to impress Diane, and even saves a beached whale.

40. A Titleist golf ball. Kramer hit a "hole-in-one." He was practicing his golf swing by hitting balls into the ocean.

41. Architect.

42. He had sex with the office cleaning lady on his desk. When pushed for a serious relationship, George bribes her with an irregular cashmere sweater. Unpleased with the offering, she told his supervisor about their dalliance.

43. George claimed he was applying for a salesman position at Vandelay Industries, and used Jerry's home phone as the contact number. When Kramer botched the plan, George resorted to dating the agency reps daughter. She dumped George after two dates, so then he promised the rep a personal meeting with Keith Hernandez.

44. Ray McKigney. He could have had any woman in the world but none compared to the beauty of his own hand, which became his one true love. Eventually the muscles became so constricted from overuse and permanently locked into a deformed claw.

45. Assistant to the Traveling Secretary.

46.   Ada. She was hired because George wanted someone with whom he had no physical attraction. He went for total efficiency and ability. Naturally, after three days he found these characteristics alluring, and they had sex on the office floor (in the thralls of passion he promised her a raise).

47.   George pretended to be handicapped. He felt justified because his whole life he has been handicapped and he never had an advantage over anyone, including the handicapped.

48.   The Human Fund.

49.   The test is when another man makes "it" (penis) move.

50.   He utilizes the "leave behind." He purposely leaves some personal effect in her apartment, which becomes the perfect excuse for another meeting or date.

51.   Blind. He could let his appearance and household decline, and a good-looking blind woman would never know she is too good for him.

52.   Buck Naked.

George (Jason Alexander) at the newsstand with Kramer (Michael Richards).

53. Mango.

54. Susan Ross. She died after licking 200 wedding invitations that contained a toxic substance commonly found in cheap adhesives.

55. Seven. Honoring Mickey Mantle (it was his New York Yankee jersey number).

Chapter Four

Cosmo Kramer

Questions

1. Why did Kramer first learn sign language?

2. At age 17, Kramer ran away from home. Where did he go?

3. Why did Kramer switch from silk jockey underwear to boxer shorts?

4. What was Kramer's mother's name?

5. One of his mother's boyfriends owned a special garment with magical powers, what was it?

6.   Kramer eventually traded the magical jacket for what illegal product?

7.   What are Kramer's two alias names?

8.   What name would Kramer like to give to his child?

9.   When Jerry's artist girlfriend painted Kramer's portrait, what is the title of the painting?

10.   What is Kramer's worst addiction?

11.   During a weekend vacation in the Hamptons, Kramer was busted for what illegal activity?

12.   During an AIDS charity walk, what did Kramer do that upset the other walkers?

13.   Why did Kramer get to sit next to Mel Torme at a charity event?

14.   Where did Kramer work when he finally had a 9-5 job, and what so troubling about him being fired?

A portrait of Kramer (Michael Richards).

15. Which Miss America contestant hired Kramer as a personal consultant?

16. When Kramer adopted a one-mile stretch of highway, what did he do to create driving chaos?

17. What Scrabble word did Kramer invent to assist Jerry's mother in a game against her son?

18. What was the name of Kramer's ventriloquist dummy?

19. Kramer nearly went pro in what sport?

20. What was the name of Kramer's caddy, and who helped Kramer take 6 strokes off his game?

21. What New York Yankee legend did Kramer punch in the mouth during a baseball fantasy camp?

22. When the health club pool becomes overcrowded, where does Kramer go to swim?

23. What store is the only place where Kramer will buy fresh fruit?

24. What is Kramer's favorite fruit?

25. When he rents a video, Kramer relies upon which store employee to recommend the best movies to watch?

26. Who is Kramer's favorite singer?

27. Where does Kramer shop to get most of his vintage garments?

28. Kramer changed his sleep schedule to 20 minutes every 3 hours after reading whose biography?

29. Kramer's phone number is mistaken by many people for which entertainment-related business?

30. Which business locates across the street from Kramer's apartment, and uses red flashing neon signs?

31. Kramer was the sole holder of a spare set of keys to whose apartment?

32. Where was the final hiding place for Kramer's strong box key, and how did he retrieve it?

33. What career aspirations did Kramer have as a child?

34. What ended Kramer's career as a tennis ball boy?

35. What is the name of Kramer's corporation?

36. What was the title of the book Kramer authored?

37. Kramer "won" a Tony Award for which theatrical stage production?

38. After a 12-year strike is settled, Kramer returns to work for which company, and why does he return to the picket line?

39. Why was Kramer fired as a department store Santa?

40. When Kramer operates a handsome cab ride business, what was the name of his horse?

41. What was Kramer's only line in a Woody Allen film?

42. What is the title to Kramer's movie treatment?

43. What actor did Kramer think would be perfect for his movie treatment?

44. What television series hired Kramer to play the part of a secretary to the show's star?

45. Kramer was an underwear model for which company, and what ended his career?

46. When Kramer is hired by Mount Sinai Hospital to portray various maladies, what disease caused him to be typecasted?

47. What word was on the novelty license plate that was accidentally issued to Kramer?

48. What was the name of the cologne fragrance that Kramer invented?

49. When Kramer discovered that his chicken was a rooster, what did he name it, and what was its special skill?

50. What does Kramer want inscribed on his tombstone?

51. Who did Kramer select as the executor to his will?

52. When ill, who will Kramer consult instead of a medical doctor?

53. Kramer has a standing engagement to get married to whom?

54. Which movie star gave her telephone number to Kramer, and why didn't he call?

55. What word is used to describe why women are irresistibly attracted to Kramer?

56. When Kramer found his soul mate (Pam), who did he utilize as a modern-day Cyrano de Bergerac?

57. Which famous New York Mets star does Kramer hate, and why?

58. What is Kramer's favorite sexual position, and why?

59. What name does Kramer use when he calls a phone sex hotline, and who is his favorite phone sex woman?

Answers

1. When he was 8 years old, a deaf cousin lived with the family for a year.

2. Sweden.

3. Because he was diagnosed with a low sperm count. He hated boxer because he was flipping and flopping all over the place. According to Kramer, his boys need a house!

4. Babs.

5. A jacket. It possessed magical powers over women.

6. Cuban cigars.

7. H.E. Pennypacker and Martin (or Peter) Van Nostrand.

8. Isosceles.

9. *The Kramer.*

Kramer (Michael Richards) smoking a cigar.

10. Gambling. He has lost money at casinos, race track, basketball, fat content of yogurt, arrival and departures of airline flights, and the infamous masturbation contest.

11. Lobster poaching.

12. He refused to wear a ribbon.

13. He was mistaken as mentally challenged by the head of AMCA (Able Mentally Challenged Adults) and invited to the event.

14. Kramer worked at Brandt-Leland investment when he was accidentally mistaken as an employee. Even though he was never hired or paid, Kramer was fired because the boss did not like his work.

15. Miss Rhode Island.

16. He removed the lane reflectors and painted over white-dashed lines to create a 2-lane comfort cruise.

17. Quone. He insisted that they needed a medical dictionary to prove it was a real word.

18. Mr. Marbles.

19. Golfing.

20. Stan the Caddy, and Mona, Susan Ross' lesbian lover, helped Kramer's swing to improve his game.

21. Mickey Mantle.

22.   East River. Although it is the most heavily-trafficked, overly-contaminated waterway on the Eastern seaboard, Kramer points out that technically Norfolk has more gross tonnage.

23.   Joe's Market.

24.   Oregon Mackinaw peach.

25.   Gene.

26.   Bette Midler.

27.   Rudy's Antique Boutique.

28.   Leonardo Da Vinci.

29.   Movie Fone. Kramer begins dispensing movie information to all his callers by pretending to be an automated phone service.

30.   Kenny Rogers Roasters. The lights prevent Kramer from sleeping, and the cones in his eyes were all screwed up (all he could see was a giant red sun shaped like a chicken).

31. Jerry.

32. He hid the key in the neighbor's pet food dish. He retrieved it by digging up the carcass of the dead pet (it died after swallowing the key).

33. Fireman. He dreamed of steering the back of the hook and ladder. Another childhood dream was to be a trucker and hit the road in an 18-wheeler.

34. While retrieving a ball during a match, he accidentally tackled Monica Seles.

35. Kramerica Industries.

36. *The Coffee Table Book of Coffee Tables.*

37. *Scarsdale Surprise.*

38. H & H Bagels. He returned to the picket line when the boss refused to give him the day off to celebrate Festivus.

39. He was dispersing communist propaganda to the children.

40. Rusty.

41. "These pretzels are making me thirsty."

42. "The Keys."

43. Fred Savage, former TV star in "The Wonder Years."

44. "Murphy Brown," starring Candice Bergen.

45. Calvin Klein. Kramer's modeling career ended when the magazine advertisement exposed his genitalia.

46. Gonorrhea.

47. ASSMAN.

48. The Beach. However, Calvin Klein stole the idea and began selling a fragrance called The Ocean.

49. The rooster was named Little Jerry Seinfeld. Its special skill was cockfighting.

Jerry (Jerry Seinfeld), Kramer (Michael Richards), and George (Jason Alexander) celebrate Kramer's release from jail.

50.   "Man's best friend."

51.   Elaine. Because she is a calculating, cold-hearted businesswoman, and when dirty work needs to be done, she does not mind stepping on a few throats.

52.   An herbalist for routine surgery, and a veterinarian for severe coughs (Kramer wants someone who can cure a lizard, chicken, pig, and frog all in the same day).

---

53. Elaine. If neither one is married by 2044, they agreed to get married.

54. Uma Thurman. She put her number on a dry cleaning stub, but his hand lotion smudged the ink.

55. Kavorka, which means "the lure of the animal."

56. Newman.

57. Keith Hernandez because he spit at Kramer after a baseball game (Mets-Phillies, June 14, 1987).

58. Kramer prefers the bottom so the woman has to do all the work.

59. Andre. His favorite phone sex woman is Erica (Jerry's girlfriend).

Chapter Five

Elaine Benes

Questions

1. What is Elaine's middle name?

2. In what city was Elaine raised as a child?

3. What is the name of Elaine's sister?

4. What was Elaine's uncle's connection to the John F. Kennedy assassination?

5. What is Elaine's IQ?

6.   Who took Elaine's photo for a Christmas card, and what was wrong with the picture?

7.   When George complained that he never received a Christmas card, how did Elaine make it up to him?

8.   After the Christmas card mishap, what was Elaine's new office nickname?

9.   Elaine took an aerobics class at the health club just so she could be in the same class as what celebrity?

10.   When Elaine volunteered to be a senior citizen's companion, what physical deformity did she have that freaked out Elaine?

11.   What was the name of the Chinese deliveryman who sued for damaged, claiming that Elaine crossed against the light?

12.   When Gail Cunningham began publicly discussing Elaine's footwear, what brand of shoes was she wearing?

13.   What did Elaine do to avoid speaking with the Pendant Publishing limousine driver?

Elaine Benes (Julia Louis-Dreyfus).

14.   Elaine is allergic to what animal?

15.   What is Elaine's favorite professional baseball team?

16.   From which restaurant does Elaine order Chinese food, and why was she blacklisted by the owner?

17.   What alcoholic drink caused Elaine to reveal other people's secrets?

18. What is Elaine's favorite movie?

19. According to Elaine, when renting movies at the video store, which employee had the best recommendations?

20. Elaine wrote a script for which successful television sitcom?

21. What pastry does Elaine prefer to take as a gift for the host of a dinner party?

22. Who is Elaine's Lex Luther? (Hint: A childhood friend who stole Elaine's boyfriend and never wears a bra.)

23. What did Elaine give as a birthday present to Sue Ellen Mischke?

24. Where did Elaine attend College?

25. To impress a Russian author, what did Elaine claim to be the original title for Tolstoy's book, *War and Peace*?

26. Which boyfriend did Elaine discard over his failure to use an exclamation point on a note?

27. What was the name of Elaine's boss at Pendant Publishing?

28. When Elaine and Mr. Lippman created a partnership, what was the name of their bakery business?

29. When Elaine worked as a personal assistant to a millionaire, what was her employer's name?

30. Mr. Pitt thought that Elaine resembled which former first lady?

31. When Elaine became President of J. Peterman, what was the first garment she designed and marketed?

32. As company president, Elaine loses all respect when she engages in what activity at the company party?

33. When Elaine suffers from sugar withdrawals at work, what pastry does she secretly consume?

34. When Elaine was failed her company drug test, what caused a positive test for opium?

35. When Elaine submitted a cartoon for publication, she actually plagiarized what cartoon?

36. When she discovered it was being taken off the market, Elaine purchased the final 60 units of which contraceptive product?

37. What word was given to describe why Jewish men were attracted to Elaine?

38. According to Elaine, who is the most unattractive world leader of all time?

39. What astonishing fact did Elaine reveal about her relationship with Jerry?

40. When Elaine's boyfriend (Roy) undergoes splenectomy surgery, what falls into the incision?

41. Elaine once dated a salesperson because he could get her a discount on an imported Nicole Miller dress. How did she exact revenge when she discovered he never ordered the dress?

42. What was the title to the song that saxophonist John Germaine wrote for Elaine?

43. What was the name of Elaine's mimbo (male bimbo) boyfriend, and why did they break up?

44. After "waiting out" the breakup of Beth and David Lookner, what comforting phrase did Elaine use to console him?

45. When Jake Jamel was rushed to the hospital after a car accident, what did Elaine do that caused them to break up?

46. Who was obsessed with Elaine and had a shrine of her pictures plastered across his apartment wall?

47. Elaine wanted which boyfriend to change his name, and why?

48. What was the name of Elaine's communist boyfriend?

49. What was the name of Elaine's elderly boyfriend who suffered a stroke moments before her breakup?

50. Elaine's boyfriend Brett was enthralled by what song (it was his song, and he would not share it with her)?

51. What song did Elaine propose to be "their song," but Brett refused?

52. When Elaine dated Alan Mercer (the bad breaker-upper), how did she end her relationship with him?

Answers

1. Marie.

2. Towson, Maryland.

3. Gail.

4. Her uncle worked at the book depository with Lee Harvey Oswald. When her uncle stated the President was shot, Oswald winked and said he was going to catch a movie.

5. 145.

6. Kramer. Her nipple was exposed. However, she liked it so much that she used a nippleless version for her health club ID.

7. She shoved his head between her breasts and said, "You wanted a Christmas card? There you got one."

8. Nip.

Elaine (Julia Louis-Dreyfus) dancing badly, as George (Jason Alexander) watches.

9.   John F. Kennedy, Jr.

10.   Mrs. Oliver had a huge football-shaped goiter on her neck.

11.   Ping.

12.   Botticelli.

13.   She pretended to be deaf.

14.   Cats.

15.   Baltimore Orioles.

16.   Hop Sings. Elaine was blacklisted because she refused to pay for a meal she did not order.

17.   Schnapps.

18.   *Shaft.*

19.   Vincent.

20.   "Murphy Brown."

21.   Chocolate babka.

22.   Sue Ellen Mischke.

23.   A bra. Sue Ellen wore it as a blouse, and it became a fashion success.

24.   Tufts University. It was her safety school.

25. *War: What Is It Good For?* Jerry told her this as a joke, but she thought he was serious and embarrassed herself in front of her boss.

26. Jake Jarmel. The note stated that Elaine's friend Myra was having a baby.

27. Mr. Lippman.

28. Top of the Muffin to You!

29. Justin Pitt.

30. Jacqueline Kennedy Onassis.

31. Urban Sombrero. It combined the spirit of Old Mexico with big city panache.

32. Dancing. Her dance moves were described as a full-body dry heave set to music.

33. A wedding cake in J. Peterman's refrigerator. It was the cake from King Edward VIII and Wallis Simpson's wedding.

Elaine (Julia Louis-Dreyfus) brushing salt off pretzels for Mr. Pitt (Ian Abercrombie).

34.   Poppy seed muffins.

35.   Ziggy. Her cartoon has a pig standing in line at the complaint department, and he says, "I wish I was taller."

36.   Today Sponge. Thereafter all sex partners were screened to determine if they were "sponge-worthy."

37.   Shiksappeal.

38.   Charles de Gaulle.

39.   She faked every orgasm. Naturally, Jerry wanted one more chance.

40.   A Junior Mint. Kramer and Jerry were observing the surgery. When Kramer kept offering the candy, Jerry shoved his hand and the mint sails into the incision.

41.   She cut his long mane of hair and sold it to make a wig.

42.   "Hot and Heavy."

43.   Tony. Elaine insisted she did not date Tony because of his looks, but dumped him after his face became disfigured in a rock climbing accident.

44.   "I'm there for you."

45.   She stopped to buy Jujyfruit candy before visiting him in the hospital.

46.   Crazy Joe Davola.

47.   Joel Rifkin. He had the same name as one of the worst serial killers in New York history.

48.   Ned Isakoff. Elaine had him blacklisted at Hop Sings (she named names).

49.   Owen March, a prominent author and essayist.

50.   "Desperado" by the Eagles.

51.   "Witchy Woman" by the Eagles.

52.   She stabbed him in the forehead with a fork. He claimed her head was too big for her body, which happened to go well with that bump on her nose.

Chapter Six

Newman

Questions

1. What was Newman's occupation?

2. Newman's route was nearly what sports stadium?

3. What was the most famous piece of postal memorabilia that Newman ever owned, and what happened to it?

4. Newman and Kramer used a postal vehicle for what money-making scheme?

5. What was the name of the millennium party that was co-hosted by Newman and Kramer?

Newman (Wayne Knight) talking with Kramer (Michael Richards).

6.   Who does Newman consider to be his soul mate?

7.   Newman would forsake Elaine's sexual advances once because he was in love with whom?

8.   Newman donated blood so which person could get a transfusion?

9.   Who hired Newman to deliver a calzone to work every day?

---

10. When Newman did a cannonball in the pool, who did he knock unconscious (and refuse to provide CPR)?

11. Newman and Jerry attended what major sporting event in 1995?

12. What woman did Newman dump, who later dated Jerry?

13. Newman discovered Jerry making out with a Jewish girl during which movie?

14. Why was Newman's car impounded?

15. Newman used his Hong Kong postal worker contacts so Kramer could import what transportation device (to start a business)?

16. Newman was called in to eat what bakery-reject food from Elaine's business?

Answers

1. Postal carrier.

2. Yankee Stadium.

3. Newman possessed the mail bag of David Berkowitz, the Son of Sam killer. Kramer convinced Newman to use the bag as collateral for a gambling bet.

4. Bottle deposit returns. They were taking a truckload of bottles to Michigan to return for the deposit.

5. Newmannium.

6. Elaine.

7. Svetlana. Newman told Elaine he was in love with another woman who belonged to another man.

8. Jerry.

9. George.

Newman (Wayne Knight) guzzling soda.

10.   Ramon, the pool guy. He was Jerry's needy acquaintance who wanted to do everything together.

11.   The Superbowl.

12.   Margaret. Jerry couldn't handle the fact that she wasn't good enough for Newman.

13.   *Schindler's List.*

14.   Unpaid parking tickets.

15.   Rickshaw.

16.   Muffin stumps.

Chapter Seven

Jerry's Parents

Questions

1.   What are the names of Jerry's parents?

2.   The Seinfelds had how many children?

3.   What caused Morty's back problems?

4.   When it comes to purchasing airline tickets, Morty proudly boasts about what personal record?

5.   Morty admitted to shoplifting batteries, so how does he justify the act?

6. According to Morty, what was the most wonderful and thoughtful thing that Jerry had ever done for him?

7. When the Seinfelds thought Jerry was broke (he bounced a check at the bodega), what did they do to make some quick cash?

8. Who purchased the Seinfelds Cadillac?

9. What special writing utensil did Jack Klompus insist upon giving to Jerry?

10. What was Morty's occupation for nearly 40 years?

11. What was the name of the raincoat that Morty designed?

12. In 1990, the Seinfelds retired and moved to what location?

13. What political position did Morty hold at the retirement community?

14. Why was Morty impeached as Condo Association President?

Jerry's dad (Barney Martin) in his son's apartment.

15. Who was the strongest man living in the retirement community?

16. When Morty wanted to be condo president (but couldn't because of his prior impeachment), who did he want to act as his puppet leader?

17. Morty is displeased with the quality of television, so what is the only show he will watch?

Answers

1.   Morty and Helen.

2.   Two. Jerry and an unnamed daughter.

3.   Sleeping on a convertible sofa.

4.   He never paid full-fare for an airline ticket.

5.   According to Morty, it's not stealing if it's something you need.

6.   Jerry bought him "The World's Greatest Dad" t-shirt.

7.   They sold their $22,000 Cadillac for $6,000.

8.   Jack Klompus.

9.   Astronaut pen.

10.   Selling raincoats.

Jerry's mom (Liz Sheridan) in her son's apartment.

11. The Executive, a beltless trench coat. It was a fashion disaster.

12. Del Boca Vista in Florida.

13. President of the Condo Association.

14. He was accused of embezzlement after flaunting his new $22,000 Cadillac. No one believed that Jerry could afford it (after all, they saw his act).

15.   Izzy Mandelbaum. He was 80 years old.

16.   Kramer.

17.   "Xena, The Warrior Princess."

Chapter Eight

George's Parents

Questions

1.   What were George's parents' names?

2.   The Costanzas had how many children?

2.   Jerry's father was an avid collector of which periodical?

3.   Frank has only one flawed issue of this periodical, which one is flawed and why?

4.   Which member of the Costanza household had a specially designed undergarment?

George (Jason Alexander) in the middle of a screaming match between his parents, Estelle (Estelle Harris) and Frank (Jerry Stiller).

5.   What prompted Frank to visit the proctologist?

6.   What relaxation technique did Frank use to relieve high blood pressure?

7.   For which war did Frank serve and fight on behalf of the US military?

8.   Which branch of the military was Frank a member, and what were his military duties?

9.   While stationed overseas, Frank had a love affair with a woman. What caused the romance to end?

10. Frank loved automobiles, and owned what type of muscle car?

11. For which volunteer organization was Frank once an award-winning member? Why was he stripped of his Silver Circle Award?

12. What holiday did Frank invent in retaliation to the commercial and religious aspects of Christmas?

13. What are some of the special events and decorations associated with this holiday?

14. Estelle always wanted George to be more like which childhood neighbor?

15. What automobile did Frank purchase that caused the other children to tease George?

16. When Frank converted George's childhood bedroom, what did he name the billiard parlor?

17.   Why do the Costanzas sleep in separate beds?

18.   What was the "move" that Frank claims he invented?

19.   When the Costanzas separated, what cosmetic surgery did Estelle have performed?

20.   During the separation, who romantically pursued Estelle (hint: he was a bra manufacturer)?

21.   What was the name of Frank's cousin and childhood companion who lived in Italy?

Answers

1.   Frank and Estelle.

2.   Two. George and an unnamed brother who impregnated a girl named Pauline.

2.   Frank Costanza collected every edition of *TV Guide*.

3.   The edition with Al Roker on the cover (volume 41, number 31). Elaine lost in on the subway, and then dripped gyro juice on the replacement copy.

4.   Frank Costanza. The men in his family were known for having enormously large breasts.

5.   He accidentally fell on corkscrew pasta (Kramer's fusilli pasta statue of Jerry). The odds were a million-to-one.

6.   Frank used the "Serenity Now" relaxation technique.

7.   Korean War.

8. Frank was a member of the Army. He was a cook for the Fighting 103rd.

9. Frank refused to remove his shoes at her parent's house. A fight ensued and the relationship ended. Frank was self-conscious about a foot odor problem.

10. 1968 G.T.O.

11. Knights of Columbus. He was accused of parking in a handicap parking space. Of course, George was the actual culprit.

12. Festivus.

13. There was an undecorated aluminum pole to use as a tree, during dinner there was the "airing of grievances" (where family members discuss the disappointments in each other), and finally the "feats of strength" competition.

14. Lloyd Braun.

15. LeCar.

16. The Place to Be.

Frank Costanza (Jerry Stiller) arguing an issue.

17.   Estelle has jimmy arms (i.e., her arms flail and hit during sleep).

18.   The "stop-short" move. While driving in an automobile, the driver brakes hard and then uses his right hand to brace the passenger (and cop-a-feel).

19.   An eye-job.

20.   Sid Farkus.

21.   Carlo.

Chapter Nine

Family, Friends, Neighbors

Questions

1. Which family member is only person that George has to "kiss hello?"

2. George once dated his first cousin, what was her name?

3. According to George, the Costanza name is synonymous with what term?

4. What was the name of George's neighbor who repaired automobiles?

The Soup Nazi (Larry Thomas).

5. George had a nonsexual male crush on which one of Elaine's boyfriends?

6. George does not believe he received an appropriate apology from whom (the man was going through the AA 12-Step Program)?

7. Kramer's neighbor had a pet parrot, what was its name?

8. What does Kramer's friend Mickey do that causes other actors to ostracize him?

9. What is the nickname of the restaurant owner who befriends Kramer and gives Elaine an armoire?

10. Who karate-kicked Kramer in the head and threatened to put the kibosh on Jerry?

11. Bob Cobb is an orchestra conductor, but what name does he prefer to be called?

12. What was the name of the lawyer who represented Kramer in several cases?

13. Kramer dated a clothing designer, what garment was her claim to fame?

14. Elaine's senior citizen companion, Mrs. Oliver, had a romantic relationship with which world figure?

15. Who invited Elaine to travel with him to Tuscany, Italy for a vacation?

16. Which one of Elaine's neighbors has a cable access show where he reveals private conversations on air?

17. Elaine considered it "level-jumping" when Stan and Myra asked her to be what?

18.   Kramer forbade which girlfriend to speak with Elaine, and why?

19.   Which one of Elaine's friends is heiress to the O'Henry candy bar fortune?

20.   Why did Sue Ellen Mischke call off her wedding?

21.   Which one of Elaine's friends always gave Jerry a "kiss hello"?

22.   Gillian (Elaine's friend, and a one-time girlfriend of Jerry), is best remember for what physical feature?

23.   Which one of Elaine's boyfriends is best remembered as being "Bizarro Jerry," and what were the names of his friend's?

28.   What was the name of the psychotic mail room employee that Elaine promoted out of fear?

29.   When using the "dating loophole," Todd Gack wagered a dinner with Elaine that involved which actor and movie?

Elaine (Julia Louis-Dreyfus) is caught between her real world friends and her Bizarro world friends.

30. Elaine accidentally dated a man who always referred to himself in the first person, what was his name?

31. Which friend always assigned tasks for people to perform at his party?

32. Which restauranteur did not wash his hands after using the restroom?

33.	The Mandelbaum family (i.e., "It's go time!"), owned what restaurant?

34.	Susan Ross' friend, Eathan, was the wig master for which theater touring company?

Answers

1.   Aunt Celia.

2.   Rhisa. George dated her to enrage his parents when they refused to speak to him. Rhisa thought they had a real future together.

3.   Quitter. His father and grandfather were quitters, and he was raised to give up.

4.   Pop Lazzari.

5.   Tony. He was a pretty-boy until a rock climbing accident disfigured his face.

6.   Jason "Stanky" Hanke. Jason refused to loan George a sweater out of fear that George's large bulbous head would stretch the neck hole.

7.   Fredo.

8.   He wears lifts in his shoes.

Sue Ellen Mischke (Brenda Strong) wearing a bra as a blouse.

9.   The Soup Nazi.

10.   Crazy Joe Davola.

11.   Maestro.

12.   Jackie Chiles.

13.   The Puffy Shirt.

14.   Mahatma Gandhi.

15.   Maestro.

16.   Rabbi Kirschbaum.

17.   Godparent for their son, Steven.

18.   Noreen. Elaine was a bad influence. She convinced Noreen to join the Army, and then go AWOL, and influenced the breakup with two boyfriends (the high-talker, Dan, and the long-talker, Paul).

19.   Sue Ellen Mischke.

Elaine spying on Jerry's girlfriend (Teri Hatcher).

20.   She found out that Elaine slept with her fiancé, Peter (or Pinter, his Hindu name).

21.   Wendy, a physical therapist.

22.   Man hands.

23.   Kevin. His friends were Gene, Feldman (a neighbor), and Vargas (a friend). They were the Bizarro World counterparts for George, Kramer, and Newman, and behaved the exact opposite of people in Jerry's World.

28.   Eddie Sherman. He wore army fatigues and recited psychotic stories.

29.   Todd Gack bet Elaine that Dustin Hoffman was in the movie *Star Wars*.

30.   Jimmy.

31.   Joe Mayo.

32.   Poppie.

33. Magic Pan Restaurants.

34. *Joseph and the Amazing Technicolor Dreamcoat.*

Chapter Ten

Memorable Recurring Roles

Questions

1. What was the name of Susan Ross' college roommate?

2. What philosophical wisdom did Jerry quote when speaking at headstone placing for Susan Ross?

3. How did the Ross family honor their daughter after her death?

4. Whatever happened to the Ross' cherished cabin in upstate New York?

5. Elaine's boss, Mr. Pitt, loved which cartoon character?

Attorney Jackie Chiles (Phil Morris) listening to Kramer discuss a potential lawsuit.

6.   What oldies song did Elaine identify in a contest so Mr. Pitt could partake in the Macy's Thanksgiving Day Parade?

7.   What item did J. Peterman want Elaine to purchase at the Southeby auction?

8.   What was the title to J. Peterman's autobiography?

9.   When J. Peterman authored his autobiography, whose life did he use as inspiration?

10.   What were David Puddy's two occupations?

11. What was David Puddy's favorite hockey team?

12. How did David Puddy show support for his team?

13. What type of music is pre-set on David Puddy's car radio?

14. What was Russell Dalrymple's occupation?

15. What organization did Russell Dalrymple join to earn Elaine's respect?

16. How did Russell Dalrymple die?

17. What was Lloyd Braun's political occupation?

18. What was Lloyd Braun's "brilliant" idea (he got from Elaine) that ultimately caused Mayor Dinkins to lose the election?

Answers

1.   Sally.

2.   Jerry was quoting, *Star Trek II: The Wrath of Khan*, when exalting that Susan was not really dead if they found a way to remember her.

3.   They started the Susan Ross Foundation.

4.   Kramer burned it to the ground when a cigar he left un-attended fell off the mantle and ignited newspapers.

5.   Kramer. Peterman pays $750 for the stories.

6.   Woody Woodpecker.

7.   "Next Stop Pottersville."

8.   John F. Kennedy's Presidential golf clubs.

9.   *No Placket Required.*

Hack comedian Bania (Steve Hytner) reveals he is dating Jerry's girlfriend's mentor.

10.   Automobile mechanic and salesperson.

11.   New Jersey Devils.

12.   He painted his face to resemble a devil, or painted a letter on his chest (along with his friends) to spell out the word D-E-V-I-L-S.

13.   Christian rock.

14.   President of NBC.

---

15.   Greenpeace.

16.   He supposedly drowns at sea during a Greenpeace activity.

17.   Assistant to New York City mayor David Dinkins.

18.   To have everyone in New York City wear name tags to create a friendlier, small-town atmosphere.

CPSIA information can be obtained
at www.ICGtesting.com
Printed in the USA
LVOW01s1420290916
506591LV00002B/90/P